I0108128

FOX P2

FOX P2
©2014 BY Russell Buker

All rights reserved. No part of this book may be reproduced without the express, written consent of the author.

Published by the Piscataqua Press
An imprint of RiverRun Bookstore, Inc
142 Fleet St. | Portsmouth, NH | 03801

www.piscataquapress.com
www.riverrunbookstore.com

Printed in the United States of America

ISBN: 978-939739-41-4

FOX P2

RUSSELL BUKER

Dedicated to David Cluff–

who will be one of the few to notice

About the Author

Russell Buker recently retired from Shead High School where he taught English and Creative Writing. He has also coachedfor many years: football, baseball, basketball and tennis

Russell has had numerous poems accepted in many publications in the U.S. and in Canada: The Antigonish Review, The Windrow Anthology, The Cape Breton Collection, Pottersfield Press, Goose River Anthology, Portland Press Poetry Section, The Aurorean, Felt Sun, The Aputamkan Review, River Muse, Germ, Page& Spine, Maine writes anthology, Crack the Spine. Russell has also served on the board of editors and written book reviews for Off the Coast Review.

Also by Russell Buker:

Powdermill Pond
Stalled Portage
Stone Cove
NOH
Frenzied Acquaintances
So As It Semed Me
Final Mask
Deposition LXX11
Markings
Nomine Mutado
Coincidence as his collaborator
Piezo

Forward

It feels naïve but how does one address his work? Never again will I believe what I have said as I have already been to that enriching construction of riverside identity, a stranger, visitor of doing, of being a writer in residence everywhere but in an academic milieu. Also, as I write this, I can not believe that I wrapped up this book, my thirteenth, a short year ago: myths to rational thought described by myths in what Samuel Taylor Coleridge has coined as a willing suspension of disbelief and by my still being a writer I am more than suspect even at this advanced age.

Table of Contents

In the Fall Air

bees awaken
bloated with weed
pollen, shaken,
freed from mating
they suck on clouds
in shorter light

aware that wasps
are new hinges of hell
and safely home
blare who dat there
shuffling my comb
bear be gone, dog gone

Trial

Why risk the possible
loss
of an all importunate
arm

where one can be
crazed
beyond liquefaction,
solace

Vision is definitely not
the same
minus any future dead-
ends,

outside seems not to
move
but naming my footsteps,
roll

of die, even though, for
now,
I am retracing my
steps

without dignity,
not to a random end-

less noise now at the
other
end of the designer
leash

because my speed of
light
keeps changing on
me

and in the progressions of
rain
storms, heavy down
pours

are not the time
to take the time

to gather all my foot-
steps
into the one that
counts

Salzburg

OK that does it
please.
Your words are
so
sad and wise she
pleaded
as I asked, on
paper,
why didn't Sophocles
save
me some, a gulp,
swig
anything for now?

Two
words collide and
I'm
drawn to the calligraphy's
s
while embracing pand-
ering
arthritis' mud bath.
When
in the hell did wondering
Walt
Whitman slide off to
leaving

me mostly alone
in
the middle of a circle
of
clean shaven kids
half
of whom are not wearing

gowns
and caps so they must
have
already graduated for
the
first time in their lives

RUSSELL BUKER

When

My plan for every day to
live or die and every mistake's
crammed in the poor car

When I find that I can not
find you anymore
in lands new stomach-ache,

or blue forget-me-nots
that dared so brightly
among testy trees, and

yellow-eyed, brown iris,
my water, my nutrients.
Be gone foreign flower

for with my imagination
I must make a sole
run for the lengthening sun

no sanctuary Arsinoe
my needles will burn
down through your roots

if I want to or seed
catalogues promise borders,
More control, more color

Say

that you knew me during my
spending
spree. That I have spent my
life
away, not just in small
change
either, although only you
counted
how many pennies clung
to
in the clear ether of day
for
thoughts, because the multiple
times
idled and torn from the time's
fabric

eventually had to be rent
from
those neat, curved hooks
on your white wall and
rendered
to crinkle in a trash can-
plastic
trash can that allowed
no
ferment, no seepage

worse
yet was having to
pay,
once again, for a huge
truck
to haul that bent copper
garbage

to an even larger air
filled,
cost efficient void

I have

been standing out here in
darkness,
want to show you some-
thing-
no one loves me in this
heat.
A man of his rust cloth
should
have no physical labor,
loaves
of bread, maybe, but
remember
they abandoned me
always
on grey city streets in the
hope
I could finally forget who
you
or I were even at Lunch's
Bagels.
Worse, whatever we were
talking
about and why that older
waitress
slipped me all her night's
tip
money and held my
hand
forever until those loose
echoes
heated up between us
in
the advancing twilight.
Hurry
she said before John Pawn

closes
and you're unable to re-coin
your,
our- brass name plate

Beach Cottage

The cottage we rented
now
empty except for me.
Swatting
mosquitoes I walk the
walk
without the grace of the
cat
crossing the path

No, I'm covered, as
usual,
in white beach sand-
the white
page with sharp tips-
I
always step away from
dream
posed , scattered thought

reflecting from cat's grey
fur
with the blankness of
paper
pressed to an ear where
an
invisible sea roar rolls
abundant
vowels among rocks

and standing gulls
quiet
in their own dreamy,
quiet
pose that at least gets

reflected
while I stumble along
back
to the vacant cottage

whose own whiteness
swallows
the staring sand and me
into
a cloudy refrigerated,
steady
hum that floats itself
out
an open, shade-less window

Thin

I love new feelings of thinness
with
dark pushing silent hands
around
my straining ears, leaves, as
though
I, too, am mere half grass

trying to do the right thing-

Standing on the uneven
plane
of this spring's planted
field
I reach out for the single
star
that calls down tonight's

barren
darkness and listen to the
whole
field slow to silence with the
final
expiration of stored sunlit
ashes

trying to do the right thing

Wait

Walt was the one
that showed
us how to list

but this will not
take as
long for you.

If I could but
get into
your corpus callosum

with a trickle
of energy
I could show you

your past and future:
where behind
all shadows you smell

death and any movement
is your
inelegant father's

apparition seeking
a way out
careful to leave some

laughter, shrugging shoulders,
ink drops
and arrows pointing up

or down for an
uneasy audience
out of its own body

The Buzz

Binary flight,
beacons of red,
random escapes,

Templars of war,
arrows of intent
on rival humming

birds: aerials, landings,
foxholes already dug
on sweetened freedom.

Many are called
mother Mary in
lots free-for-all

Thank You Robert Bridges
.....for saving GMHopkins

Early fog sweeps
lazily
as car winds slowly
up
the lane where
no one
has to leave for
work

Gulf Stream loco-
motoring
north past the Sargasso
Station,
boarding passengers,
fuel
and we scan the dull
waters

of everywhere wondering
how
to halt a line of thought:
what
if anything could
we
do if this, our world,
were

to crumble mightily
while
we wait and want
another.
What to do to plan,
make
our living again in
case

we have to. Yes
have
to figure out how
to
utilize strands of rope,
needle-
sharp crystals already flung
away.

RUSSELL BUKER

Without

Oh my God, I can
see
you shaking your
head.
without my ubiquitous
mirror
this could be it:
you
glimpse me in third
trimester
or last quarter as
moon
shining throughout it's
stages
and often on blank sky.

When old age brightens
beyond
our long-necked wine
bottles,
well educated in darkness
to
brilliant in distilled drop
light,
clear then humid,
soggy,
just like everyone
else.
Oh my Lord, can't I
see
me shaking my head.

Sloth

My mouth is
dry
we are all alone
momentarily

You are a sloth
big
round, wet
body

Mara's mundane
enticing
earth touching
mudra

crossing the night
road
bright blue
eyed

always, it seems, in
commuter's
way and why
not

in this humid
heat
all is possible
inside

the hum of an
auto-
mobile's under-
carriage

Medusa

No word yet
out
of the frigid east.
Algol
or our demon star
still
blinks, seemingly
bereft
of her numbing magic,
shines
through our whole
universe
probably as a
warning
that black matter,
her
origin, matters
even
in our attics where
bats,
rejection slips
mould
onto our spines
while
other universes
pile
upon themselves
for
a better look

You should

not have to call.
The wind
has me, once again,
noding,
as I sit on my
porch
waiting morning light
with
a purring kitten in my
lap.
It seems I am
always
responsible for something
or
other. The trees are with
me
on this, the wind and
I
have similar, soft
hands
holding silent claws
in
pre dawn sharpness.

This

is not
about what has
been
lost or declined but
gained

just when I most
felt
like screaming my-
self
into an anonymous

retirement-even
my
students have moved
on
to other rationalizations

other
than me and see
I
no longer have to
be

the enterprise, whole
sponsor
for anyone/thing
who
did not know what

I
was doing with all
that
reddish tape wrapped
around

legs and ankles making
it
difficult to feed those
wild,
boarish razorbacks that

were
scavenging my loose,
blue
veins for anything
sweet

Perhaps

Of all the
outages
in this risky
business,
unhappy ring-
tones

Perhaps it was
nothing,
a light noise,
shallow
dash of memory
lost

A stone's moan,
perhaps,
the words mean
nothing
yet I keep
calling

them for you
in
the hope they
will
flare from the
sun

of our yesterdays,
scorch
the very wires
connecting
me to you, you
to

me and all those
others
who sit so
patiently
in the connecting
grid

that has gone
suddenly
quiet, flailing
in
the cold curl's
smolder

I remember now
how
lovely your legs
when
the swelling went
down

Shopping List

And the cat follows
me
movin on moving
down
waxy aisles shopping

that refrain crowds our
ears

Always a branch
between
us- you wont remember
me
with all these industrial
twigs,
green with mimic and
your
swallowing hard-
for
me to hide behind

while
fracturing your earth
letting
the next generation
fend

for themselves and I
will

eventually take these too
tall
trees allowing sun to bear
down,
down and crack those fracked,

fertile
soils and what was to be
with
wings of dust whereto,
unto
whom with moving on

still my privilege and
my
cat will follow.

Everything

Everything flowering bows
down
in the rain

the geese have come
early
this year

Everything was early
this
year again

my room reminds
me
of a dry wadi

valley of unrelenting
light
few shadows

the haven which receives
more
of his light

where I find myself
becoming
afraid again

in this land of small
shadows
smaller insects

my memory's unable
to follow
immersed thoroughly

and no air to breathe
the way
thunderstorms rob

the surrounding air
of it's
oxygen again

even the fall loons
are
forced to find

shelter congregating
in the
corner of the lake

murmuring their hello's
soothing
ancient songs

T-Rex

This spring's evanescence,
fragrance
wet earth provides with
another
sighting of the returning
birds

Arranging the blaze
almost
wish for summer's end,
though
I realize my supply
dwindles,

no torpor here, glowering
rivals
about to return to stage
before
ocean crossing unaware their
habitat

has dried considerably.
The half
ounce of fat necessary
to cross
will be hard won even
hibernating

Our hope they will not
rapidly
alter their DNA's
return
their history's gain and
become

tiny Trochilidae Rex
swarming
with new/old beaks of
teeth
gnashing their barracuda
attacks

flashes of red dripping
off
lips smacking contentedly
in
the strange, old light of
dawn.

Book

There is no APP for this
Not one line
Sewn on grateful
Page sings to us

How could this be
You ask so softly

Most of what we've
Ever read: the rain,
The thunder, mid-winter
Clues opened shivers

Why would this be
You ask so softly

The last piece of arable
Land granted from
Gentle, wet, lava hiss
Sea boiling in the dark

What will happen to me
And all our neat domesticity

Battery energized by sun
Yet step less Babel tower
 Lies silent in my hand
Except for time and day

This howling wind, saucy,
Does not time its' advisorary

FOX P2

Golden eyed dogs creep
Closer ignoring beer cans strewn
On our lawn, alpha signings
Fade with sun and mist

Will we obtain another privy,
Salted book of readability

Tamtamsis

In the dark night
waves break
onto this island

I was asleep on our
treeless dome until
diagonal souls

of becoming mothers
and we became one.
Talking dreamily

we enjoin in the
beginning of a world.
Minds so near self

see indistinctly
forms of light
not of this world.

Wind freshens southerly
water fills up
in the night

Pagan

How pagan I am
breathing back at
this silence of trees

during this fall for
the first time
full of nothing

having screamed
back at the wind's
varying speeds

learned vowelings
with such straight
linear lines and now

becoming a pebble
of dust looking to rest
in the flash of a star

gone long before my
first breath, yes
way long before

Reluctant

Cold
bumblebee's rapid
feel
of Foxgloves penance.

Bells
peal so faintly
in
September's wind

that I return to colder
house,
watch out my oblong
window.

Artificial
boundaries categorized
with
extra, waning light-

blue
moon's reluctance still
lingers
into this morning

These bones

are like ivories
if
touched in damp
night

blue bones winnow
grit
out of panting air,
pearls

drop out silently,
become
rigid, hoboed, then
waft

into iridescent
alphabets
hidden in the shining
solitude

of bivalves that are
clamped
shut in the tide's
absence

We Are

so crowded in by
hedge-
rows between cabins and
forest,
where night never
can
leave, between us and
the road
nor allow vision of that
road;
yet, I distinctly hear cars,
trucks,
or children on their bikes,
sounds
that murmur we are here,
are
moving about, unlike a
recreational
boat on the water with
passengers
waving, slowly at first,
to
anyone caught in their
square,
squeeze of a yard

It

is not such a
good
thing that I
always
found I had to do:
gnawing
on a bone's darkened
shadow

It

had to be a thought,
fiction:
I could have sworn
that
I heard someone
say,
"you are a brackish
man"

I had fooled around,
prodded
with a stick in
order
to ascertain the
origin,
of a small brackish
clump

in the small stream
behind
my dwarf house.
"Oh

no," I mentally replied
to
no one in particular,
"I've

only patted her
arm
ever so lightly
as
I walked her and
her
dog home that quiet
night

for I am more
than
aware of the autism
such
a high concentration
of salt
can accomplish wholly,
awkwardly."

Perfect

Today is perfect:
over-
cast, no visible
distractions

This is a waiting
game,
more obscure than
Jude,

I have cast my
web-
page with a beautiful
voice-

roll and now wedge
it
near the riffle of
fast

water and wait
before
reeling back in
above

the rounded rocks
where
the water makes its
best

music while the bottom,
persistent,
urges my feet sea-
ward

with a strong, glacial
energy
I ignore and cast
again.

Outside

it is completely
dark
playful reflections
taken
for granted are
gone

A lone street light
at
the other lake end
wobbles
in unseen rising
mist-

Ruth who really
had
nowhere else to
go,
settling in stranger's
laps-

the dark will rest
your
eyes father said-
a somber
emblem already in
the dark

of my mind's black-
I remember
the sparkle and will
look
for him in the returning
light

where everyone comes
to me
along the waves and it's
difficult
to differentiate Ruth from
father

And Still

Straining to keep up
with my cantor's syntax
remembering nothing
does not really matter

And still it rains
through the soft
platter's porous cryptic
of a loon chick-

mother's filled beak
repaired having
left for winters sea-

So it was that rainy
day when mother
left for what I
hoped was a galaxy

expedition and the fright
I hear in that loon's
call was mine also

I had to learn too
before pond shell ice
circled around my feet
making me easy prey

for tree-bound eagles
or the light footed fox
who would tug all day
if he had to, could

Summer's

long exposure
so trainable

This new mist
from warm lake

weeps off fall
windows, wrapping

brittle trees,
closing the lane

with such slow,
grey swallow

all we can do
is listen to the

withering of summer
bristling, wrestling change

Chase

I am not going
to chase anyone

in this wind-
neither with it

or against it- what
with its dusty breath

stopping fingers that
lay cause and effect

deeply imbedded while
still unsure where or

how far it has gone
when it's gone on

Mine

and the tree's
survival kit

was always
much sun

One pulse
growing

genetically
Strobis and Bukered

along
Rue Celestial

Tell us
if there is
anything else:

It is not
that I feel

as covergent
as I used to,

admiration
for that-

knowing you
can't reciprocate

only sense
my nearness

as threat,
Relish your

branches, nest
syllables wind-

wended my way
yesterday, all day

Imbricates

is how my
earth always stays,
weighs the same

voiced over or
thinking out loud
I roll along

clustered, watching
those in distant
games using their

3 energy systems:
point my finger
at the man selling

corn, dogs or ice
cream and slide settle,
unaware but conscious,

that time on the field
is meaningless and
quickly running out

In

autumn/fall,
half's last
half

of summer,
the years warm
half,

riots from
green prison's
hold

with movement,
wind, felt/ seen
leaving.

Standing alone
all this while
moiled

movement felt
in my veins,
in

my ears with
compass points
lost

in this back
lit dark as
star

souls drift
down in their
excited

migration. I
no longer
hear

myself wonder
if clouds are
clouds

James Dickey
(Balm to Ben Greer)

Buoyant now with who
we are now in his
clutch, a sear of energy,
smell of cheap whiskey's
ignition, we knew it
could not last, would
ash up in the wind
replacing the heat
with history's char

you had to give up
whiskey in the fiber
before they took your
daughter and every night
you roared through dream:
could not say anything;
words had become balls
of silent cotton piling up,
snow, around two blank

dots, daughters eyes really,
as you wanted to tell them,
" May all your landings
be as soft and never run
out of super superlatives
reading my stuff while
reaching for the comma,
semicolon; the colon:
and finally the period.

Autumn in New England

Flowers born questioning
their birth,
for who was my father?
I started
as seed without gumshoe
boots
for the wet, soggy soil

And why this precious rage
of growth,
will the cooling down
matter,
will there be enough rest
after this-
a moment of play stoppage-

who will advertise my quiet
necessities:
Rimbaud's taking off his
clothes again-
five years bursting for his
mother's delight,
with birds quarreling

so sweetly as last night's
wind comes
regularly to this garden.
Where are you? I need
you to
bear these finals of many
final frosts

Sisyphus

Con cen trate,
concentrate not
on your bearing task

Although your left
hand is not as strong
as the right one

remember to allow
body's compensation
by leading with your

right foot when working
the left side , short
step and twist a little

your two fantasies
spill from your wet
brow and down your chest

what would happen if
you did reach the top
and stopped everything

for the view. Would
you dare to push that
stone down hill again

would that be the same
as leaving the stone at
the bottom and walking up

would leaving the stone and
moving on, where ever,
tarnish my long legend

do you want this fame
of burst intentions
down such a smooth trail

of regretful insight that
draws me back to the
heaviness of settling stone

Split Rock (Pessikapskiyak)

Dictate
how simple, too simple
really:
just go to the annals
of
the Canon Presses and
then
chose to become editor.

Meanwhile beside the horse-shoe
pit
and the government wharf
sits
the rock, split so long ago
no one
remembers the quakes of
frosts
shoved down a cleavage
pane
every spring with it's
sounds
attended reverently, more and
more,
as we gathered to watch schools
of fish
swirling in the bay feeding,
escaping
their own violent roe-woe
by
predators we hope to prey
upon

Snow in the Forecast

We were, to say the
least, always happy
in our ageless town
of shaken winters,
snow falling down

now our arc of heaven
it's inverted plastic
bubble gathers snow
as the flopped village
slowly divests itself

We can not see nor
imagine heavenly worst
throes for those who
reside there now and
those who still want to

Fall

What have I been doing,
done,
trusting, as it were, in
the beauty
of all fall deciduous trees:
where
it seems I am walking
among
myself again without
dieing

most of the leaves have
fallen:
my fantasies of varying
color
lie inert in the hard
rain,
not quite comfortable
yet
but looking to the ground
as

somewhat of a savior
while I groan, not of loss,
wondering
where the children have
left
the rake and wheelbarrow
the last
time this happened as brown
oak
replaces raked Birch and Maple

Compression

cold caffeine again
while
I contemplate
what
to make of a day
that's
in the way, when
obviously
anticipation is the key
that
looks for built up facial
smiles
amid growls to be
left
alone, pining, for
sunset
to fill this vacuum of
vacuous
daylight until a sleep
where
nothing moves and
tomcats
prowl feral factories'
shh
matter of factually

En Pointe

To clear the mind and
arrive somewhere gasping,
grasping, the enterprise
accomplished, for now,
as the rationalized mind-

mind of the downy wood-
pecker flying away from
my plate glass window's
surprising and painful
rebuke seriously distracted

from an avenue of flight
that had seemed so clear
from the feeding station's
maddening full compliment
of greedy, feeding birds

Do not mention Kafka's
Palestine or La Belle Reve
but it is true I am always,
always away from here,
weg-von-hier,

Review

I hung my head, lower
and lower,
as she explained me to me:

Your songs are crap, non
tenured,
remember that, remember

as that is what is good,
good about them-
She told me

this on my last visit to
the hospital- Look,
you're getting old, I see

strings fraying, falling
into your neck crevasses-
I wanted to ask if she saw

anything through those thick
glasses- and I can not keep
the whine in the cellar.

It has climbed the stairs
and yesterday's conjuring
of gaudy beads

on silken threads that
wound
around my cocooned

youth: run along, run along
frugal fun
go AWAY I hear the doorknob

turning

Just a Note

silent blue jays
seem to stand guard
in the large tree

days have become shorter
again. No one worries-
they think me flabby-

Oh yes, the gloves
are now off.
Even these wind engined

brown leaves of oak
are resembling shapes
in this solitude that stretches

into the talkative nights
seeking prehensile comprehension,
fragrance of wisdom

or the vastness of reply
that somehow fears its
ambiguous algorithms

will not suffice, tower tumble
while two legged desert
dogs practice barking

at circling dark, looming
vultures dropping into
their history of cleanliness

Crito and the Cock
.....Sophecles yew

more black stones
in the urn than
white ones

and I fretting over
the payment of a
chicken

lie down at home
on my back while
my feet grow numb

and thank you my
dearest friend for
closing my eyes

putting stones in
them for I have
seen enough

Pleasant

dreams beside the road
passing
no one in that long line
between
hero and fool everyone
asks
if these dreams contemplate
drifting
away in fog's wet drizzle
or
stoop-bending down under
early
frosting or padding away
behind
the giant visiting cat

silence- even the word
breaks
the plane of articulated
vision.
Word, oh, I guess Pound
was
so right to be suspicious of
what
we have done to their meanings,
moving
from awe(joy) from the unspeaking
silence
to the sharp bark of danger or
communal
blessings. Hardwired into our

greed
with the shunned General lying
in
the glade during thunder
storms
with an erection to learn
what
it is all about: meaning,
love
reflected in shining boots
no
matter the external weather
or
storms within, without
love.

Locks

it is the randomness
that
overpowers, coming
home
to find your door wide
open

war is hell Ma Belle

Doors are locked for
a reason
my father intoned
every
night until one day,
broad
daylight, he came home
to
the open door. I'm
losing
it he thought aloud

war is hell, Ma belle

staring from his couch
while
mother smiled in her
dresser
mirror holding a new
note
found in her drawer

mais ce n'est pas la guerre

Mid November

while I stand on the shore
burning
brush in the silent morning
wind
of mid November's first
light
changing mauve birch
into
candlestick white a fishing
white
breasted loon drifts in and
around
camouflaging in reflected
trees:
swimming the way our words
are
sought, changed to make
us
fishermen in the forests of
this
dawn's uncertain waters.

Thanksgiving

by now I do not
have
to remember where oh
where
I have put anything

and I love standing on
my
porch in pre dawn's
dark.
the gold-less finch have

come
back standing in growls,
whistles
to say whether or not
all

should have a look
or
how sweet you, Raven's,
lacking
a so long renders my face,

long
outside the slot of your
now,
apparently unshareable,
acceptable

noise garnering turns, twists
only
in my own custom Carnival's
fading
plumage and quirky steps

Psychiatrists

I certainly could
have kept going
but Saturn and Venus
have stopped

and are looking
over their shoulders
as the quick footed
moon passes them

on its way to
sealing perigee
I could ask
what it wants

other than watching
me without enveloping
the pity and pathos
Wallace Stevens assumed

for it too hesitates
then readies to hop
over florid Mars into
less friendly apogee

RUSSELL BUKER

I arise

later and later every day.
In spite of its shortness

the fall is the scariest
time for all of us:

lake water, exhausted,
from two day wind-

lashing lies calmly
talking to its own

reflections about
living on borrowed air

In this time of eating,
being eaten, where even

the rain seems to be
eating into our solitary

contrails with deranged, plodding
stomach as we slog slowly,

evaporate from the page's
autographs we transcribed

and how can we know,
being dead, if anything we

borrowed still blows in these
careful fall winds

Improbable Me

earth
rock & dust
molten lava
asteroids or comets
bring water
lightning
right place, right time
sequencing
under oil blob
material
first cell-at da
chemical instructions
cloned cells
big whoop
this all sounds rapid fire
but it is not still for that
little while we visited
our possible selves
assume an importance
for you are lost with-
out me to scorn

And we ran straight to War
Sargon killed his peasants
to feed his army while
Ahuitzotl butchered
20,000 to appease 1,000
gods, especially Tenocha
to insure his daylight And
we all remember Blod's
odor of hydrogen cyanide
or the rotten London Fog
60 years ago killing 12,000.
this, too, sounds rapid fire

Even though

a strong
swimmer, I
learned
watching waves
every
wave
crash onto
Boon Island
rocks
while beneath
there was
more death-
dealing
swimming around
awaiting
rock severed
morsels,
tid-bits,
while I
watched
with only
thin, knee-
high
gunwales
up to my
knees
Thankfully the traps were baited,
Thankfully the motor started
and we left Boon to its older
memories. Thankfully injuries
prevented me from returning
from battle and having to learn
how to become angry at friends,
family without killing them.
This surely was rapid fire.

The cat

and I
peer so
disinterestedly
at scraggly-eyed
strangers
and birds
bouncing
off
our windows
with an
almost
amazing
impunity
or concussion
leaving only
a scaly headstone,
feather,
to mark their
interrupted
journey.

After the Rain

my breath, unseen at
this
time of the year,
keeps going back to
sky
which swallows it easily
keeping
my universe's interpretation
relevant
to my usual landscapes
but
somewhere out there we
probably
have mingled, touching and
talking
so effortlessly that I am
reminded
of the wizened, soft spoken
lady
at the glaring pawn-shop
telling
me she would like to give
me
more-sigh- much more

Enter

slow giants, squinting
to memorize
this fog's life-made
fluid
from dreams slow
frieze
in the minds' iced
convolutions

gone the sharp angles,
cutting
edges of early winter
prompting
blood circulating from
core's
geometric transmission
back

to all eyes filtered in this
cold
heat, where ghostly swirls
rest
between where we thought
we were
and are in January's early
thaw.

In the Dark

This sightless morning
I stand alone,
having just fed
the birds, to feel
the silence of a
first snow drift
down to me and sense
my intuition pushing
against the diminishing
space I used to own

It suddenly occurs
that I have only
dented the universe
by a dust's width-

Space shared with
day time clouds
night's star shine
blank paper-
now the wonder how
soon this will
emulate my last act,
horizontal pen, as
I and my aura
are enveloped

Blues for Alice(1939) Clark Coolidge
Riff
and all that Jazz

unrecorded and thereby single on the night
when you get in on a try,
you have been asked to solo

and the others, group, will follow
as You play around on familiar
ground giving the others, group,

a chase in a riff and they love you
for it and never look back only exclaim
that Mutha knows his Parker bird

fear not, no need to explain the joy
of a slighter than slight voice-
emeralds flight in the evergreen

gives us our daily bread, tres-
pass energy, while the drum lies
flat on its back- while my audience

keeps tapping on the wrong beat, horses
running honestly for pasture, strong-
legged mares young again, happiness

RUSSELL BUKER

You have

perspired profusely and
in this moist, Etruscan heat
you have taken the history
out of me and now wish me
to mate with an erotic, red-
thighed, marble statue on this
last day of vacation where
there is nothing to do but
watch someone peel and eat
peaches, forgetting completely
that you have always eaten
them skin and all pre touring
these tatters of antiquity

A Dry

A dry, cold, westerly
wind
winds around our
land
making all remember
how
the sparks flew in
summer

moonlight dries
allowing
the impression
wind
has stopped our
shaking,
and can vest in
lee

A thing apart

will go on clicking
   until the batteries wear.

One still point came
   and went with a remote

camera's silent flash. I
   now know one thing

lurking while I sleep.
   Laser panic registers

in the unassuming
   feral cats secret vision.

Forever barbarian and
   always, on the outskirts

of cuddly chic while living
   off all that splendid

solitary scenery that has
   vacation roads built to

accommodate smooth
   urban trawlers. The cats

and I eke through night
   wounds on laser powered

red flashes of battery re-
   generation, giving and taking,

even in the blank, furriest,
   darkest-dark

Cold thoughts

Please do not tell
me
about the birds already
gone.
Nothing
stirs at all in this
much
cold. A light
blush
on the snow
lights
the way for
eyes
that miss nothing
and
weigh upon covered
shoulders
while I hastily cast
remnants
of reveillonner's
wishful
thinking. Now I attempt,
being
at once lighter and
heavier,
the stupid way I
go,
to retrace opposite
steps
without veering
into
the heavy boot swallowing
snow.

Christmas Storm

Coyote noise floods across
the lake
while I, never more alone,
am
supposed to have only one
place
to go in my advanced age
yet
with closing, arthritic hands,
lumpy
heart I still love my cocoon
in
the storm, hiding and reappearing
behind
long drapes of early morning

I do not know how to tell
you
this feeling- there is no
language
only emotion or today's
imagination
as I shovel the new snow-
children
really, who have come back
as
snowflakes playful in the
streaky
wisps of a moving storm-
oblivious
of anything but discovery

My fear is that some might
be
hurt, again, by the rumble
steel
makes as I part the snow to
make
a path for myself wherever
I
am going through such a storm.
They
adapt to all new friends so
quickly
in piles of friendship that
will
remain with me until Spring's

sun washes us back to our lakes
and we swim, silent snowflakes

I'll forget

today's ecstasies when the
wind
dies. Freed beyond being
re-embered

I tried, tired listening to
breeze
increase, to hell with mere
words

How I long for you to
send
one restless red-wet
kiss

via the internet copier
machine's
lasered photo of your
lips

Nor
do I have the patience
any
longer for one long

drawn
out Hollywood version
that
is supposed to encompass

the rest of my future:
my
celluloid, figment-ed
lifetime

Fly By

This day could fly by
planet energies
afford extra speed,
momentum

doctors will stop
dead in their
tracks while I
make a career

of spinning out of
control, bothering
a hungry eagle
feeding on a dead fox

a subscription for
loneliness for sure
I do not crave fox
or its winter pelt

www.ingramcontent.com/pod-product-compliance
Lightning Source LLC
Chambersburg PA
CBHW051735040426
42447CB00008B/1150

*9 7 8 1 9 3 9 7 3 9 4 1 4 *